ECHOES
OF
CONSCIENCE

Kenn Amaechi Jnr.

Orange Taste

ECHOES OF CONSCIENCE

Kenn Amaechi Jnr.

Kenn Amaechi Jnr.

Copyright ©2015 Kenn Amaechi Jnr.

ISBN: 978-978-952-001-5

All rights reserved.
No part of this book may be reproduced, distributed, stored in a retrieval system or transmitted, in any form or by any means, electronic, electrostatic, magnetic tape, mechanical, photocopying, recording or otherwise without prior written permission from the Publisher.
For information about permission to reproduce selections from this book, write to info@wrr.ng
National Library of Nigeria Cataloguing-in-Publication Data

Printed and Published in Nigeria by:

Words Rhymes & Rhythm Limited
Suite C309, Global Plaza Plot 366, Obafemi Awolowo Way, Jabi District, Abuja, Nigeria.
08169027757, 08060109295
www.wrr.ng

Orange Taste

CONTENTS

DEDICATION	6
PREFACE	7
REIGN OF VAMPIRES	12
MASQUERADES	14
AFTER THE INSANITY	16
MESSIAH	18
BURNING NATION	21
ADIEU GENERAL	23
KEN	25
OUR LEADERS	30
VOX POPULI…	32
ASSEMBLY OF THIEFS	35
They are yesterday's men	35
DO NOT THROW	36
BABA SEGE	38
WHEN SHALL WE LEARN	41
LETS TALK	43
LISTEN	45
ABOMINATIONS	46
AFRICA	51
OUR FATHER	56
NAKED SONG	57
ECHOES OF THE TIMES	60
IF THEY KNOW	62

BOUND TO BONDAGE 66
THEY ARE NOT SHADOWS 68
LORDS OF THE MANOR 70
BORN TROWEY 71
HUNGER, PAINS AND MISERY 74
GIDAN VIDEO 76
THE INQUEST 78
ACADEMIC RAZZMATAZZ 81
BROKEN 85
BAKASSI 86
ECHOES OF CONSCIENCE 88
OGBANJE 89
NGIGE 91
LONG LIVE THE KING 93
THE VERDICT 95
ASO ROCKS IS FALLING 96
TO YOU 98
MY COUNTRY FINE 99
LOOT AND GO 101
MY MISSING MUSE 102
TURAKI WEPT 103
WE KNOW 104
TAKE THE OATH 106
LET'S MOVE FORWARD AGAIN 107
GLORY PLACE 108
I SEE HOPE 110
I HAVE A DREAM 111
YOU LOST YOUR GROOVE 112
THE QUIET TEMPEST 114

CRY, BELOVED SENIOR SCIENCE POTISKUM YOBE STATE..115
SACRIFICE...117
IT SHALL PASS OVER: A Poem for PMB 118

DEDICATION

To Thomas Aquinas Nwanze
who is a first witness to the flame that ignited
my imaginations for greater expectations in life.
Thanks For believing in me .

Kenn Amaechi Jnr.

PREFACE

"The man died who keep silent in the face of oppression and tyranny"
— **Prof. Wole Soyinka**

This literary work is a creation of stirred inspirations emanating from the realities inherent in daily situations and vicissitudes of life. The poems are a cocktail of soul searching and emotionally charged variables recollected in solemn tranquility.

Reading through, the reader is bound to discover that the poems are not willfully wrapped in some esoteric language or style, rather they are conceptualized and written in a form, which makes the ideas and messages behind them easy to comprehend for the general reader who is…the average literate person and the ordinary folks in Nigeria and beyond. The poems are also satirically spiced and pungently exhilarating with a lot of pun to wit. The style just like the varieties of the poems does not fall within any particular hitherto existing conventional or traditional poetic genre.

The theme of the poems is varied; however, a common and consistent consanguinity binds the poems. The poet is fundamentally critical of the socio-economic, political and moral disequilibria, dislocations and cataclysms in Nigeria and Africa in general with a clear disdain for Western Powers "over lordship" over African affairs and interest.

The overriding and consistent theme of the poems is lamentations, which is a product of positive hatred, hatred against social inequality, hatred against political irresponsibility hatred against-moral cataclysm, hatred against the profligate and apathetic elite in the Nigerian society.

Some of the poems are mere poetic statements, but written in a philosophical manner that readily stirs deep emotions and is consciously crafted to be thought provoking. The poems move with the earth and the earth rotates round it in unison.

Orange Taste

On the whole, I intend the collection of Echoes of Conscience to criticize, but just as well to reveal, rejuvenate and effervescently to touch the heart of the reader in a mystic way. The poems flow in a childlike honesty and simplicity with a tapestry that is enthralling, because it is appealing.

– Kenn Amaechi Jnr. (November 2005)

Kenn Amaechi Jnr.

In these poems, Ken has evinced the challenges and opportunities of my country. He has, in few interesting lines, laid bare the language with which we speak about fear, about patriotism and about the future. Ken has shown that we are but a nation yet to harness its full potential.

His words are a reflection of what he is; a passionate optimist whose voice always says "let build new dreams…And Iroko height hopes", these were excerpts from Ken's poem 'Tell them'. They are a reflection of a man I have known for over a decade. A man that has travelled the east and west of this country; has seen the south and north of our territorial frontiers. And like a sailor, he is home to tell the story of his voyage.

In letters, he has again awakened the strands of my reflections about Nigeria, as every line sparks mixed emotions about the story of nation in transition, a people so resilient and a conviction that suppresses every fear.

Abubakar Kagu PhD
University of Sussex
United Kingdom

The collections, ECHOES OF CONSCIENCE, echoed all the fears and concerns I had for my dear country Nigeria before I set out to the United States to further my education. Thought provoking and written from the purity of heart, it is very obvious that ken has passed through the labyrinths of Nigeria's social and political dislocations.

His poetic collections are a true testament of our collective experiences. I see this poetic collection as yet another reminder that as a country and a society we live on the edges of life because our shared desire for economic, political, religious, social, and cultural liberty is yet to be made perfect. The poet has given us hope, that in all these chaos we can one day rise above the temperamental weaknesses that draw back our awakening and reach that greater good. Ken we are proud of you, well done!

Nwamaka Anaza
Assistant Professor and Educator
Southern ILLINOIS University Carbondale, U.S.A

Orange Taste

Kenn Amaechi's 'Echoes of Conscience' is a creative, thought-provoking and soul searching anthology of poems. His style portrays a poet conscious of his environment and one with an eye for the emancipation of a people trapped in a quagmire of indecision.
I recommend unreservedly, this anthology for all those seeking answers to questions of hope and aspiration and to those who dream of a better society
Augustine Arimoro
LLB Maiduguri, LLM (Commercial Law) Derby
Solicitor and Advocate
PhD Candidate London

I have recommended the high level of thinking of the author, very philosophical that reminds me of ibn Khaldun, one of the best Arabian poets of his time. Each line I read is so precise and though provoking not so surprised it emanated from an aspiring member of the most learned profession.
Kamal Alh Daud
Senior Lecturer, Department of Shari'a Law
University of Maiduguri

Ken Amaechi Jr has a revolution in his heart and this shows in the poems he has penned
A burning desire not only to paint the gray arrears of the lives we live, but to push us to aspire to loftier ideals.
Chika Jones Onwuasoanya
Renowned spoken word poet
co-author of 'VERSES FROM THE NIGER'

Kenn Amaechi Jnr.

*Conscience is an
Open wound
Only truth
Can heal.*

(Othman Dan Fodio)

Orange Taste

REIGN OF VAMPIRES

They are virulent vampires
Façade of decent beings
Arenaid in dog-eat-dog jungle junks
To devour and destroy.

Catch your breath
As you behold the monster's venom
Spats out of its beakers
Stench of virulent vomit
In a stagnated pregnancy
From unbridled protruding belly's jail.
Bribery and corruption cries the belly
Urges delivery, but nature impedes
Because abomination is never condoned.
The masses seek redress
To punch and purge
By Caesarian section.
Beware!
Of their beautiful feathers
Flirting wings to impress you
Their radiance a scourge on the flesh.

If
    You walk on their footsteps
    You live under their wings
    You eat and drink their lust
    You sing and dance to their rhythms
You stand and listen to their obscenities
An ancient traditional belief
Binds you to their fraternity
In servitude.
Doomed Into a contract with evil
To taste paradise in hell.
My people wail and weep
For carnivorous sits on mercy throne
Salient in death splendors
Sucking the honey and honeycombs.

Kenn Amaechi Jnr.

Our bodies are famished
Our blood heated
Our flesh food to vampires
Our life in the illus of vampires
Our destiny their toy to toddle

Where are the eagle and horse?
Where is the pledge and anthem?
Where is the coat of arms?
Where are the sacrosanct laws?

"When bad men combine, the good must associate, else they will fall one by one on unpiled sacrifice in a contemptible struggle" – **Edmond Burke**

**Written in 1998, during Gen. Sani Abatcha's hey days as military Head of State.

Orange Taste

MASQUERADES

   The cloud hanged
Aso rock blazes with divisive radiance
As hawks and vultures gather
To parasite on the remnants
Of their spoiled garden
This has carcase of democracy
Scattered like garbage on the land
A macabre tale of man's malevolence
Which like a roaring holocaust
Swept away a beautiful hope
Down the tunnel of grave ecstasy
Leaving us to sing the song of sorrow
So long, we prayed
That the cord
That binds us breaks apart.

   The cloud hanged
The horizon seems penetratable
For another transition to no heaven
As charlatans and masquerade
Hijack the Aso market
There everyone is a commodity
Its trademark has no name
The trademark
Is chop! Chop! And chock
It's ugly face
Scares away
Virtuous sensitivities.
They have gathered again
To water the seed of corruption
Breed nepotism and tribal markism
In our already bug infested landscape
They wear the rotten rags
Of democracy
  Ethnocracy
  Militocracy
  Diachytocracy

Kenn Amaechi Jnr.

    Nepocracy
    Deceiptocracy
Dictatocracy
    Power shiftocracy
    Compromistocracy
    Regionatocracy
    Tazarcetocracy
Theirs is the melting pot
Of political chameleonism.

"Politics must be founded on principle to make meanings; politics without principles is a social sin" – Mahatma Ghandi

**Written in 2003 at the onset of the General elections.

Orange Taste

AFTER THE INSANITY

    Let the moon rise
    From deep dark cloud
    Let the sun set
    At peak of hope
    Let stars color
    The beginning of new dreams
        After the insanity

    Let the nation sing
    For joy over our divine triumph
    Let the inglorious past
    Be confined in iron coffin
    Let purge our minds
    Of this unbelieving reality
    Of our dilapidated history
    Let wash our conscience
    Of unconscient lust
    That strangled
    The heartbeats of our existence
    And rendered us impotent
    In the glowing face of tyranny
    Let's bury the pains
    Of the holocaust
    After the insanity
    We have starred into horrifying terror
    Of the eclipse of our visions
    We have seen the humiliation
    Of men that steered the nation-ship
    We have seen the idolatry of the crown
    We have seen
    The caps insanity
        Kangaroo courts
        Set in and set up
        Have confounded us
        Into boiling silence

        We have seen

Kenn Amaechi Jnr.

The root that is our morality
We have gloomily accepted
The oracle sacrifice
We have mourned enough
For the phenomenal death
    June 12
The sacrifice that appeased the gods
    After the insanity
Now that we can still breathe unpolluted air
And take our eba unmolested
Now that we still sit
And talk our grieves out
Without frightening
Temperamental weakness
Now that we can still
Blend our irreconcilables

Now that we still
Have the fragments
Of our mentality in check
    Before we all
    Embrace insanity
Let start afresh

Let build new dreams
And iroko height hopes
That won't flinch
From the stare

To fill our heart
And heal our wounds
Let's recreate the Niger
And make fresh beginning

"The making of a new Nigerian can only be achieved by men of vision, bravery, and passion for Nigeria and not self" – Kenn Amaechi Jnr.

** Written in 1998 after the death of M.K.O Abiola and the set in of democratic transition.

MESSIAH

Our messiah come
Our hope enkindled
Trumpets were blown
to herald the coming
of the bearer of peace.

to the cross and crescent
we all trouped to offer
thanksgiving sacrifice
of triumph over
Hurricane doomsday.
We didn't wait
to see the rebirth
of a new dawn
our excitement
consumed our reasons,
    Hastily,
we buried without coffin
The menace that struck
us down to our knees
and crippled our psyche
like zombies
we forgot to
seek hibernation
against the transvestism
of darkness for light
in false route
we journeyed towards
the abyss of destruction
and despair
we metamorphosed
from giants to midgets.

The messiah constrains
Our heart beats with
His heart tricks.

Kenn Amaechi Jnr.

our messiah appears
Our sun disappears
our messiah speaks
Our Niger demarcates
like a vengeful thunder
he swept off
our heroes past
into the pit of infamy
our resources dried
we became epileptic.
Our people were bedevilled
with hypnotised trauma
we were recycled
                      from
   peace
                      to pieces
  to
    peril,
and the land quivered
the people shivered

Those that had wings
flew away to safe havens
and learnt to threw pebbles
that hanged on the air
away from the general's fortress.
those that were wingless
stood in trance
and prayed open eyed
   and counted the market days
   with their left brain
   as they lived with berthed breathe
   Those that thought they were bold
   Croaked and shouted,
   The general was dared,
   And like weeping ant
   They never lived long
   to hear the echoes
   of their voice
   as their native blood

Orange Taste

flowed in spurts
on the streets of Lagos
Ibadan and Kaduna.
Those that strayed
Were picked
one after the other
like zealot birds
that sang absent-mindedly
and crestfall
on ithier masters
fornicating garden.
Those that watched
from a distance
scampered back to nest
and sang no more
in their cocoon
they learnt to
write with their feet

sending shrapnel messages
to stillborns
    to never embrace
    khaki and dark
    goggled messiah generals.
(June 1997)
        Never.

"Power is within the grasp of even the mentally deficient. So, really, power is neither direction nor vision it is simply an ambition" – Professor Wole Soyinka

**In memory of the dark goggled General, Sani Abacha, who died on the Aso Rock throne as a maximum leader. RIP.

BURNING NATION

     Atop
The Aso rock coccon
rises an ominous flame
so fierce its burn reaches
below the hearts and souls
of the downtrodden and down below
whose vitriolic vent
has been hidden
in the now
dashed hopes of
a betrayal messiah

     A flame
Ignited
by ethnic schism
Religious bigotry
     A flame
fed by deregulated corruption
     A flame
Incensed by poverty and hunger.
     A flame
Enhanced by conscienceless greed
     A flame
fuelled
by leadership insensitivities
     A flame
spread by soaring
parasitism
cronyism
sycophancy
Idiosyncrasies
Inordinate ambitions
tazarce
hypocritism

share-in
Resource control

Orange Taste

Bakassi, OPC
APC, Egbesu boys
All have gathered
Like the dry weed
of the forest
to inflame
the Aso hilltop
    Killing,
        Assassinating
bombing
the people.

Our nation
is on fire
we called them
to build the nation
they burn the nation.

This flame,
No sea can quench
not even the benevolent
Niger and Benue rivers
can quench.

The ruins in motion
Our leaders in passion
junketing and trunketing
like a dog on heat
they fiddle and foundered
    Niger fission and filters
    In tatters
    we cart
    our destiny
    to disaster.

**Written in March 2001, after the onset of democratic government. There were several ethnic, religious and politically motivated conflicts in Nigeria as a result of the self-interest of politicians.

Kenn Amaechi Jnr.

ADIEU GENERAL

    A great general,
    A gallant soldier
       his ascent
to the throne
A messianic promise fulfilled
And the people echoed
    Alleluia!!

    Alas!
As the moon circled
The general conquered power
Sovereignty became his tool to doom
With a snap of his fingers
Undeserable species were sent to gaol
Others disappeared at midnoon
Some scampered to exile
more ascended to heaven
 lifted by rogers flying machine.

But alas!
The great general,
The alfa,
The revered,
The maximum,

was carried away
to oblivion
by the pleasure ridden
tunnel of an Indian
Angel.
An angel of death
He was cast
    cast down
to a grumbling earth
he was mourned
      mourned

Orange Taste

by a horde of chameleons
whose only remorse
was the padlocking
of the nation's treasury
by the eclipse
of the tyrant
Adieu general S. A
(June 1998)

"The tree of liberty is often watered by the blood of patriots and tyrants" – Thomas Jefferson

Kenn Amaechi Jnr.

KEN

Ken was our ken
A ken gentleman
blazing hot and strong aura
conquering life at his forties.

Ken was brave and brainy
passionate with red revolutionary
blood glittering in his eyes
Ken moves with mission
his thoughts were
the engine room
for the propagation
and the protection
of human dignity.

Ken my soul mate
In spirited devotion
To expunge traces
of man's inhumanity to man
in our weeping land.

Ken had red fire
in his fearless tongue
his finger ooze blood
from long drive with pen
to drive out death penalties
hanging against man's liberties.

Ken came
from the darkest quarters
of our light house country
his kiths and kin
lived a lifeless life
without light

without water

Orange Taste

without tarmac
without care,comfort, and contentment
without education, hospitals, and welfare
without any life line
        from the reservoir of treasure
        that lay underneath
        Their dilapidated thatch
        and bamboo houses
        which made lagging lagos a panoply of sky crappers
        an ocean of atlantic pleasures
            AND
      Abuja
their Abuja
a fallow and desolate place
turned into an
architectural masterpiece
a smiling and enchanting beauty
a heaven
for kleptomaniac looters

Ken was a lonely voice
A faint, amidst a choir
Of parasitic praise song stars
    But
Ken was our voice
In a land of voiceless choristers
Ken was our
Kind, kith and kin
Ken was a brother
Cousin and Uncle
Ken was our light
the light that
Radiate freedom.
In a land of voiceless choristers
Ken was down to earth
with us

    the downtrodden and down below
    the plundered and persecuted
    the wretched and wronged

Kenn Amaechi Jnr.

the homeless and hungry
the dream and hope builders.
Ken was
    Until
    till
hours of vultures
hours of vampires
hours of senile sensitivities
hours when no song is heard
hours when all voice is void
hours that tickles in naked darkness
hours that tickle in thieving death
    until
    till
that pit less hour
that robbed us of Ken.

they sent Ken
to the other side
of existence
They took away
Ken's body.

 But
Why, why? Oh Why?
did they snatch away ken.
    Yes we know why
Ken was a light
That shine out darkness
Ken said no to tyranny
Ken said no
to thievery and deceit
Ken was a star
that glittered amongst dims
Ken rebelled against injustice
Ken was innocent to guilt.
                        Yet

Ken was hung

Orange Taste

despite the cries for mercy
despite the emissaries of peace
despite the UN and CW missions
despite the pleas from multitudes
despite his holiness handshake
Yes his holiness in his holies
shacked for peace
for life
    Yet!!!
Ken was hanged
his bright eyes
glazing trails
for emancipation
his sharp and eloquent
voice blazing
his endearing features
blossoming.
ken
You may be out
but you are not gone
For Ken is us
we are Ken.
Ken
embrace our hug
Receive our kisses
The kisses of bliss
take our blessings
the blessing of saints
we hug you Ken passionately,
Your memories
your rock conscience
Your overwhelming principles
Your white truth and honesty
we hug thee whole.
Your grief
Our grease
Your pain
Our path
Your sorrow
Our seal

Kenn Amaechi Jnr.

Your misfortune
Our fortitude.

Ken
we can see you
in white apron,
shining,
shining
like the sun
  we can see you
   sited on the side of angels
     Happy and radiant

we can feel you
you are with us
in love and in trust
         adieu ken
             adieu peace.
(1997)

For Ken Saro Wiwa (RIP).

"He is not worthy to live, the man who hasn't found something he can die for" – Martin Luther King

***Ken Saro Wiwa was an Ogoni environmental right activist, hung by the Abacha military junta after a kangaroo trial.

Orange Taste

OUR LEADERS

Their luxury glitters
from the lax gait
of our life.
Intoxicated with blood stained
leisure of our dredge
Our lack their laugh
Our tears their tease
Our pain their peace

Our misery enkindles
their corrosive brutality
of our dignity
At the altar
Of a paper God
Yet,
They are the custodians of our life
I call them
the undertakers
of our impoverished
body and soul.

We are aboriginal slaves
serving the motherland
for Aboriginal masters.
We hew wood
and fetch water
for the light and growth
of the nation
but we never smell
the fruit of our labour
though we sing the anthem
and make the solemn pledge
we are fed only
with nectars of despondency
                deprivation
                          depression
                desolation

Kenn Amaechi Jnr.

But even if we
We are the dregs
of the nation
can't we have
the dregs of our sweat?
We cry Oh!
Motherland
Save us from the clutches
of motherland murderers.
    (April 2002)

**The forces of a capitalist society, if left unchecked, tend to make the rich richer and the poor poorer, this is the case in Nigeria

Orange Taste

VOX POPULI...

Poverty is let loose
on the streets,
hunger is driving people
to painful precipice,
starvation takes stock
of its casualties,
in file of excellent cadavers
despondency adorns
the linen contours of the faces
of our people.

We are beaten
we are battered
we are bitter

that our common wealth
is their common loot
our joint inheritance
their sole inheritance
our resources
they resources to flounder
our recovered loot
they prized settlement.

We the people
the derogated masses
inhabiting the Niger
we have been maligned
we have been cheated
we have been bamboozled
we have been deprived
we have been dispossessed

we have been excommunicated
we have been abused
we have been battered
we have been marginalized

so deeply to feel the pinch.

Those that were trusted
those to whom we freely
offered our hope and future
those that we accepted
those that we embraced
those that looked us in the eyes
and chorused 'yes' to our aspirations
those that behold our trust
and chanted like saints
> I solemnly swear
> to maintain the dignity and integrity
> to uphold justice and equity
> to turn stone to bread
> to squeeze water from rock
> to shelter the multitudes
> to quench the fire of ignorance
> to be just and fair

They derogated from their offer
Conscienceless like shylocks
as the throne of power rested on their shoulders
they now turned to massacre our will
and dumped us in the ocean of despair
> we are now orphaned
> in our motherland.
> those of us that asked for positive affirmation
> were answered with battalion of sodomite soldiers
> whose burnt offertory spits from their anus.

those that cried for security
of their life and property
where vindictively granted
a state of emergency
those that prayed to be educated
were obeisantly answered
with 17th century canons
to chop off thier arms,

Orange Taste

      cut thier legs and lash thier buttock
      for questing for life more abundant
      we the masses
      we the people
      we the down trodden
      we are beaten and bruised.
    BUT let it be known
    That when the cock crows for us
    We shall go in our mass
    To uproot
The infamous fortress
Of Aso Rock
Vox populi, vox dei.
(July, 2001)

**An oppressed people are authorized when ever they can to rise up and break their fetters.

Kenn Amaechi Jnr.

ASSEMBLY OF THIEFS

    They are yesterday's men
    Of little means
    Today's lords of the manor
    They emerged from
    Rickety weeping
    Boots and cars
    Prostrating
    Cajoling
    Begging
    Appealing
    For our assents
    To back our nascent baby
    We gave them
    our baby democracy in trust
    to bath
    but they now batter
    and our baby is thrown
    with the bath water.
    We never bargained
    For this den of cheats
    Who have assembled
    To despoil
    Our donation
    From God's generosity
    (July 2002)

"To keep a Nigerian from being corrupt is like keeping a goat from eating yam" – Obafemi Awolowo
**Written after the gale of corruption that was witnessed with the coming of democracy and the brazen display of affluence by politicians in 1999.

Orange Taste

DO NOT THROW

    Do not throw
    Into the wind
    of fiery tempers
    the umbilical cord
    of our endangered being.

    Do not throw
    to the maddening crowd
    the sacred honey
    that nourishes our existence

    Do not throw
    Into demagogue sentiments
    The Amalgamated twins
    That charms
    the pride of our nation

    Do not throw
    to conscienceless passions
    The speeches of happy remembrance
    Lest we forget
    To sing the song of life
    Song of our rebirth.
    do not throw
    into the sea of confusion
    the doves "udo" leaves
    lest they sprout
    And grow poisonous weeds

    Do not throw
Out of leper's morality
Orphans custody
To greedy dogs
Lest they shed innocent blood.
        The scare of dark days
        have cleared

the cobwebs across our eyes
In our dreams
is apple visions
waiting to shine.
Kwashiorkor
Doomed doom
Adulteress democracy
Transition to death

Don not throw
Our foundering canoe
Down the pit
Of the Niger

Baba Sege
　Do not
Throw away
Our fractured monolith.
(January 2003)

**2003 under President Olusegun Obasanjo witnessed a lot of political upheavals in Nigeria. The several ethno/religious and political conflicts threatened the existence of Nigeria.

Orange Taste

BABA SEGE

      You
promised us say
pump go dey rush
like river and stream
you said our light
go dey shine un-quenchachable
You said food go dey
Our table yanfu yanfu.
You said our pikin
go enjoy free education
You said we go live
safe and sheltered
You said we go
enjoy better health
you said loudly
you go put
sunshine and sunshade
into our life.

   Baba Sege
we hugged you
we embraced you
we believed you
we trusted you
we thought
you are with us
our kind, kith and kin
who saw all affluence
walked down the valley
of a common foe
into the shadow of death
And in whole
offered ourselves
as the living sacrifice
of redemption
And you
the sacred light

Kenn Amaechi Jnr.

of a dimmed hope

came back with
the face, body and soul
of a common convict
you were humbled like us
we saw humbled eyes
we saw your bones
ejected out from
your freckled flesh
your strain our strength
your faltering tongue
enkindled our pity
your tottering walk
gathered our sympathy
your in Jesus name
scented speech
gave us faith to carry on
your messianic demeanor
captured the essence our strugle
we filed in uberimei fidei
To unknown slaughter slap

Baba Sege!
What have you
given us in return?
Bullets and massacre in Odi
Fire and deaths in Kaduna, Abia and Kano
Ethnic cleansing in Zaki Biam
Bombs and corpse in Lagos
Umuleri and Aguleri
Have become lands
of the living death
Our land is under
siege of chaos
      hunger
      starvation
      and extinction
And you tell us
To shut up.

Orange Taste

Baba Sege
where is the hope you gave us?
where is the promise of a common wealth?
where is the water and light that won't cease?
where has our garri gone to?
where is the free education?
where is the shelter?
where is the sunshine and sunshade?
where is that hope?
baba Sege
we thank you
for putting our trust
in your trunk
we thank you
for elevating our poverty
we salute you
for distributing our common wealth
to your common fiends
in your well fed excessive council
whom you called out
to chop and drink
we thank you
for quenching
our ascendary ray of light

Baba Sege
we thank you
for showing us
that your generations
 is a
wasted generation.
        Wasting our generation.
(May 2003)

"No man is wise or honest enough to be trusted with absolute power" – Unknown

Kenn Amaechi Jnr.

WHEN SHALL WE LEARN

It's not long ago
we cried, the cries
of despondent sheep
as we filed to the slaughter-house
to be slaughtered
we shouted for salvation
our eyes gazed widely towards the sky
our ears waited patiently to
hear of miraculous eclipse of doom
our nose smelt
the odour of a nation
diseased with graft
our feet twitched Cankerworms of corruption
and angled towards
      safe abode.

We craved for time
To sweep away our miseries
but time is no one domicile
time an inpatient host
it came and hoisted
      the hogs
of our nation
and fled away.
time a pregnant traveler
that gives birth at pause,
we begot a new time
fresh, innocent and promising
with white flower in its hips
the sorrow and misery
that turneth our light
      to darkness
and made garbage
the deeds of our heroes past

  We
have defied learning

Orange Taste

and wise counsel
from the pains and trauma
of yesterdays mis-adventure
stubbornly we trek the
paths towards destruction.
And the deadly pestilence
just like the Jews of old
acted unwisely
and atoned not for their sins
in forty years of wilderness
after a freedom
from pharaonic captivity
we too just like the Jews of old
steams in obstinacy

      our youths
have become youthless
poverty alleviation has turned to
poverty ad libation
our wealth, their loot
when shall we learn?

The vultures of yesterdays
are yet not far off
      perhaps
when they time comes
when they descend on
the Aso hilltop
and scavenge on the living occupants
when the vultures come
      perhaps, yes, perhaps
      we shall all learn
      our lessons
      the Somalian way.

(May 2003)

The politicians are our problem in Nigeria.

Kenn Amaechi Jnr.

LETS TALK

Lets talk
The time is here
      Waiting
Watching patiently.

We should be talking
But many are singing
Many more are shouting
Some are dancing
Many more are musing
Some are clapping
Many more are crying
Some are laughing
Many more are wailing
The base and tenor
Has lost rhyme
Our instruments charts
Their own course
The problem is not
The choir but
The choir masters.

We should talk not about sovereignty
Lets talk
Not about oil wells
Lets talk
Not about numbers
Lets talk
Not about land size
Lets talk
Not about tribal marks
Lets talk
Not about our tongue taste
Lets talk
Not about religion
These are relics
Of past misfortune.

Orange Taste

Lets Talk
About life
Our life

Lets put our hands together
And make our life better
Lets talk about
The orphaned child
Dying of starvation
Dying of neglect
Dying of corruption
Dying of greed
Our own greed
For none is feeding the orphan
Everyone is milking the orphan
                lets talk
And put our voice
  Together
For Nigeria!

(May 2003)

"I love Nigeria and i conscientiously believe that if we can harnes and pull our resources together and respect each others peculiarity we shall achieve greatness" – Kenn Amaechi Jnr

Kenn Amaechi Jnr.

LISTEN

    Listen
If you mind
Be deaf If you must
The quarrel if any
Is not with choice but effect
For the hurricane
Chose not its victims
Neither do pestilence
Have favorites'
The hour is now
When we all should
Stand and be counted
Amongst patriots
Who stood firm
Amidst temperamental weaknesses
Of political demagogues.
(May 2003)

**Written after the 2003 general election that stared violent political sentiments in the country.

Orange Taste

ABOMINATIONS

At the white man's feet,
generations had sat
and perspired at the
magic of malevolent wisdom
scintillated from the white man's
   chameleonic tongue
its spittle, a poison
that dwarfed African giants minds
and made porridge
of our great knowledge.

Our fathers had swallowed
All the saliva
pulsating from the
white man's ephemeral indoctrinations
they had been held
spellbound and infatuated
by alien tongues
in their reverie
they lost the pearl
of home-grown wisdom.

They have taught us
what they want us to believe
they took our consciousness
to dark solitary confinement
and clouded us with unknowledge
even when we know
what they knew
and see beyond what they saw
they must be there
to direct us like sheep
and show us properly
what our eyes can't see
we had remained
faithfully under their tutelage
not graduating from

Kenn Amaechi Jnr.

a toddler to a crawler
Rather we are genealogically
and permanently baby-sitting.

Now
they claimed to have left us alone
to follow footsteps of a borrowed destiny
we thought,
we could fire our own wood
and swallow our amala
but as it is,
we can't ingeniously wood fire
our own woods for food
counting all the years
they spoon-fed us
with their educational concoctions
we ought to have metamorphosed
into masters of ourselves
yet we remain in perpetual servitude.

    though
if the truth should rain
we can see
we have dark lining
poto potoing our trek
to self-renaissance
and be part of global progress
But, the white mischief's
have permanently
clowned us into ideological whitewash
we have remained a black sheep
to be heralded by white shepherds
    But are we blind?
    We are victims
    Of self complacency
or perhaps
we have taken too much
of their concoctions
to brainwash and be cloud our reasoning.

Orange Taste

But then?
what of the growing seeds of youth
that are just sprouted and eager
to catch the baptism of nature
or, had the fathers leprosy infected the child?
Yes, the Whiteman
has devised means
to dwarf us,
even if we appear like Iroko giants
they have overloaded us
with the garbages
of overrun roman empire
and stunted us with archaic, decrepit
volumes of useless papers
to keep us subdued and moronly engaged
with puzzles and maze
of their past fancies
in Art
    Science

Technology
                Commerce
and humiliatingly
throw in our face and emotions
the means they battered
the humanity in us
and equated our genes with those of mammons
in their infamous Trans atlantic
                Transdome
                Trans death.

Lo!
today it is a new type
of voodoo and hypnotic slavery
in the name of globalisation of calabash
they chain our consciousness
to the absurdity
of their hoodwinking cultures
and displays of insolence
      their feelings and manners

Kenn Amaechi Jnr.

    their belief and ways
    their temperament and sensitivities
    though we share whisky and sandwich
    and speaks and hear their jangling tongue
    though we shuffle together in parties
    and blow off killer smoke together
    they will never let us into
    their secrets
and their light
will never shine on us
we remain permanently and parallel
apart from them
like the earth heads
and the heaven's feet.

But
must we follow their transcript
to perfect our own imaginations?
Shall we remain perpetually in search?
Whilst they rape and conquer the moon?
we watch, its reflections on the Zambezi river
they create super human machines
to cheat on the burden of labour
and have more time
for their sinitry life
we are still fighting
over the smallest fish ponds
and un-able to mend
the miming iniquities
of our wooden bed
they pride in their paw-paw colour
we crave for artificial coloration
they manufacture human dolls
and questions death's ingenuity
we are still devising means
of coercing goats to procreation
and yet can't stop
a righteous baby
from mosquito murder
the gulf

Orange Taste

     ocean
      River
of our inequality
  is kilimanjorish
  But we can capture
  our burning imagination
  like the yellow and red Asiatic skins
  we can build high mountains
  cross gulf and ocean of inventions
  and surround ourselves
  with oracled superiority
  we can proclaim their
  ways, feelings & manners
  taboo in our land
  and render their ideologies outcast
  we should do away with their junks
  their language and smell
  we should term abomination
  lets go back to black roots
  and begin afresh from the loot
  of the whiteman's lust
  and ingeniously create
  from scratch
  the dream world
  of our weary eyes.

(August 2002)

"Africa can be great if only it overcome its psychological bondage to the west, and self inflicted physical and mental laziness" – Kenn Amaechi Jnr.

Kenn Amaechi Jnr.

AFRICA

Africa
can't you see?
The dry bones
of warriors and cowards
of saint and villains
of the rich and poor
of god like leaders
of proletariats and the bourgeoisies
of the mighty and underdogs
of the professors and the profane
    All alike
in the streets
Mansions
ghettos
Bushes
Death camps
Military camps
Undergrounds gaol
Imperialist clutches
SAP Cul-de-sac
Sidewalks of death
    in
Angola
Somalia
Liberia
Algeria
Uganda
Kenya
South Africa
Nigeria
ZSierra Leone
Congo
Togo

All offsprings of Africa
in the heartland
of Africa

Orange Taste

Dear Africa
Land of my ancestors
Land of liberty
Land of freedom and freeborn
Land of peace and unity
Land of milk and honey
Land of plenteous harvest
Land of black gold.

 Oh! Africa
The land of ancient wisdom
  land of lion hearts
  land of resilient warriors
  land of peace goddess
  land of beautiful maidens
  land of sweet voices
  land of happy choruses
  land of worthy appraisals
  land of sacred justice
Oh! Africa

in your shores
  scattered
like the sand of time
  And
Innocent blood
  shed
On your sacred grounds
It foams and boils
It trails in search
of the butchers of justice

 Africa
Can't you see
Can't you feel
The god's annoyance

 Africa
Boils with the blood of orphans

Kenn Amaechi Jnr.

The blood of the victims
The victims of greed and selfishness
The victims of paralysed sit tight leaders
The victims of myopic senses
The victims of selfish aggrandisement
The victims of corruption and nepotism
The victims of ethnic cleansing
The victims of wanton accumulation
The victims of white mercenaries
The victims of borrowed ideology
The victims of misplaced priorities!
The victims of tyrants and traitors

Yeah!
Africa you can see
Africa you can feel
the vapours
    scorching
your flesh
down to the souls
of valiant ancestors
    invoking
The spirit of heroes past
of Murtala and Sankara
of Lumumba and Cabral.

    Africa!
Rise from dreamless sleep
Rise from doomed womb
Rise from dumb visions
Rise from death slumber
Rise from dry bones
Rise from dead waters
    Rise!
        Rise!
            Rise!
Like the black eagle
Unbending in the bloody wind
blowing in Africa
unflinching under the sun

Orange Taste

hat scorches the people
unscared in the rain

Can't you see
the dry bonesthat rains poverty
un-afraid of the
    voice of vampires

    Africa!
Rise
and cleanse the land
    cleanse Africa
of black vultures
    white mercenaries
    lepers hearts
    palmwine conscience
    gigolos of white imperialism
    hands that shed innocent blood
    sit tight paralysed leaders
    betrayals of trust
    voluptuous stomach
    unsympathetic sycophants
    Human parasites and bootlickers
    Bad egg diplomats

Africa:
    Mother Africa
    Rise and redeem
    The face of your world
    rise and make
    Africa proud
    Proud
that rains poverty
un-afraid of the
    voice of vampires

    Africa!
Rise

and cleanse the land
    cleanse Africa
of black vultures
    white mercenaries
    lepers hearts
    palmwine conscience
    gigolos of white imperialism
    hands that shed innocent blood
    sit tight paralysed leaders
    betrayals of trust
    voluptuous stomach
    unsympathetic sycophants
    Human parasites and bootlickers
    Bad egg diplomats

Africa:
    Mother Africa
    Rise and redeem
    The face of your world
    rise and make
    Africa proud
    Proud
of black essence.

(July 2002)

"Africa has come of age we shall no longer take decision from any extra territorial power, the destiny of Africa is in our hand to make or to mar" – Murtala Ramat Muhammed

Orange Taste

OUR FATHER

      Our father
      Who at in Washington
      Hail to thy white house
      Thy king- doom come
      They wiles be done on earth
      As it is in hellven
      Give us fools day
      Our daily terror
      And forgive us
      Your trespasses
      As we welcome your transgression
      And lead us into damnation
      But deliver us into all evil
      For theirs is the king -doom
      The power and the gory
      For ever
      And ever
      Until peace
            Is vanquished.

***Written a day after America struck Iraq for the second time under George Bush Jnr.*

Kenn Amaechi Jnr.

NAKED SONG

It is my song
It is their song
It is our song
We have sung
Suddenly sullenly
with our tongue
clipped to our teeth
our eyes padlocked
by dew of anguish
Our noses dancing
to sorrowful hearts
Our body, a laboratory
of shockwaves
Yet, we must sing
So that even in limbo
The echoes of perilous time
Shall bug in the ears
of generation unborn.

My song
has wheel and wings
every ear, its destinations
It can be seen
It can be felt
It can be touched
In the streets
Markets
Hungry homes
Deserted schools
Dome fortress
In the field of death frenzy
In the belly of hungry souls

My song
an everywhere and when song
sang by voices

Orange Taste

that have seen through
the cankerworms
above the
weeping earth.

I must sing
it's everyone's song
My song praises no one
except good virtues
My song dances not to
the gallery of deceit.

My song a hurricane
In the ears of the unjust
I must sing
So that not we all
Can be poisoned
by the double standard
of an apathetic society.

My song
Imitates no one's tongues
My song dances
to no one's tune
My song a live song
that roars out the darkness
of a perverse society.

I sing, the way I see
I sing, the way I hear
I sing, the way I feel
I sing, the way I know
the ugly and beautiful faces
of species above the earth.

My song
A friendless and foeless song
My song a sensitive song
for sensitive senses.

Kenn Amaechi Jnr.

With inkless pen
I scribe it plain
with naked voice
I sing it loud
its conscience and morality
a piece of my heart
echoing the sound
of stricken souls
seeking for peace
        justice
                equity.

My song
a woven cloth
for a naked society
a naked song
for naked souls
a naked song
for naked sensations.
My song pierces
the dark skin
of a cruel
and covetous society
My song
is a dress
to nature's
        nakedness.

(April 1997)

"Speak the truth, follow your conscience, be your self, make a difference, change your world for the better, life has no other alternative than to be lived the way you are" – **Kenn Amaechi Jnr.**

Orange Taste

ECHOES OF THE TIMES

    poverty paints
     the faces
    Of destitute children
     the weary pensioner
     the people lying sick in hospital
    the old grayed lady
    the rag-tag graduate
    the Ivory tower lecturer
    the palm wine taper
    the noisy black-smith
    the lady with protruding belly
    the policemen with the patched uniform
    the human-spectacle beggars
    the grazing animals.

Poverty every where
A covetous epidemic
In this land or ours
From the Niger down the Benue
It embraces and clutches
Famished bodies
Crippling the knees
To an early earth rest..

Breakfast and dinner
A constant battle fought and won
Every minute
On the streets
Farmland, market places,
And wage-less jobs.

Yet, body refinement eludes the flesh
And left the bones suckling out
Looking for cover
From the scouring
Pains and poverty
Poverty

Kenn Amaechi Jnr.

Sound and echoes
Loudly
On the streets, parks
Chilling at home
In market place
Choking in and out of school
Smelling in ghettos,
Shacks and hospitals
Paradox of human handicap
Spread epileptically
Everywhere, everything
Has the cold touch of poverty
We search to see
The cause of this aberration
But the seer neither the oracle
Can tell the direction
Whence it comes
Whence it goes
It stays with us
Amidst natural wealth
Our breath tickles
In suffocation and *pains*
Of the fear and sorrow of poverty
With long outstretched arm

It cuddles the emissary
In the colour of the rainbow
Rendering all spineless
That catches its
Evil spawn
Its ravages,

An
Echoes
  Of the times.

(June 2004)

"Man is born free but every where he is in chain" – Jean Jacques Rousseau

Orange Taste

IF THEY KNOW

In the streets of Zamfara
under the sun scorched desert
earth of Dutse
Treks the almajiri boy
    Barefooted.

Hungry and angry
his bowl on his head
his eyes searching
for Alhaji's leftovers
seeking for expired crumbs
And the maze of unidentified
particles of food
from mama-put trash basin
    unsuccessful
he will go to sleep
with his rag tags
under the shelter
of contaminating
    heat
        his stomach a field of acrobatics.

In the street of Onitsha
in the money-spinning empire
of Chief Okoro motor-parts shop
Inside the oga's chamber
kneeling like
a condemned criminal
his arms and legs chained
like an expired forlon
is the apprentice Nwaboy
His master wielding 20 inches
    electric cable wire
        twai
            twai
                twai

Kenn Amaechi Jnr.

Screams of terror echoes
the boy's sin
N100 deficit in sales
He ran to the Police
for justice and got
    jungstice
    which is more of jaundice
The master in suit blazers
gave the complaint and defence
the Sergeant nodding
    'Yes sir'
    'Alright sir'
'It will be done sir'
Poor boy
no education, no hope
Six years of servitude
down the drain
the fruits of his labour
Compensated with
A home
in a repulsive cell
with hard labour
for stealing nothing.
The centre of excellence
under the Oshodi bridge
creeps a young man
running away from home
He's been driven from school
for lack of school fees
forced to child labour
forced to Abuse
his back-breaking
his neck-stiffening
he ran away from home
To seek home under the bridge
from thence to join

    the band of Area boys
        OPC boys
        Bakasssi boys

Orange Taste

      Yandaba boys
to lash

on an apathetic society.
In the beautiful city of benin
roams an adolescent girl
of 16yrs old
heavy with protruding belly
impregnated by her school
PrincipalDriven away by
her guardian angel
Roaming the streets of Benin
arms folded
eyes gazing into misery
No home to go

No father for her
Still born bastard
She walks amongst shadows
She mirrors herself
She sees a depraved sShe realises her place
She realise her child
may end up in
a pit toilet
if the bastard is lucky
it may breath life
in an abandoned building
A deserted bush land
"A born trowey basterd"
  She will then become
      A master of the merchants
      the merchants in sex trade.

They are all
A spectre, a mirror
of our society
A virus of social decadence.
They are all
A spectre, a mirror
of our society

Kenn Amaechi Jnr.

A virus of social decadence.
    If only they know
    of infant relief Act
    of fundamental human right
    of the right of the child
    of act against child Abuse
    of act against child labour
    of the dignity of human life
    of the right to fair hearing
    of the right to education
of the right to shelter

    of the right to self-protection
    of sect 14 (2) of the constitution
    of sect 17 (3) of the constitution
    of the poverty alleviation programme
        if and if
        only they know.
    (October 2002)

"The God who gave us life also gave us liberty at the same time" – Thomas Jefferson

**If the almajiri system had been casted away long ago, we won't have boko haram today.

Orange Taste

BOUND TO BONDAGE

He lives
on the opposite side of life
his comfort is adjacent to conflict
his hope is a cul-de-sac
which ends with scrubs on the street
his dreams drizzles into poto-poto
As he crashes from a street bench
sleeping
resting
from physical malnutrition.

He
dwells
At the darkest quarters of the earth
bereft of life's texture and lustre
cohabiting with misery and mystery
companion of hunger and anger
Darling of pests and pestilence.

Eating-bowl on head
Short niker with square hole
perhaps by design
certainly by default
But now
his natural ventilation
that gives a comic relief
to his gloom-infested life.

Tomorrow, the Siamese twin of his
yesterday's travails
begins with the recitals of life
under the neem tree
with cold embrace
from the excruciating harmattan
biting through his body
to the limping stick
that is his

bone marrow.
From there
he move
a loner amongst multitude
a servant to servitude
a walking scepter
of social inequality
in our justice
repulsive society.

He
is but a posthumous humanity
bound to poverty
bound to squalor
bound to hunger
bound to destitution
bound to ignorance
bound to ignominy
bound to bondage.
    (1997)

"A day and hour of virtuous liberty is worth a whole eternity in bondage" – Joseph Addison

Orange Taste

THEY ARE NOT SHADOWS

    Eat not
    Shelter not
    Clothe not
Their daily creed
they incantate for life
heads bowed down,
rising with the pitch
of a sonorous song.
Thereafter
the street
will be theirs to conquer
every pathway
holds hopes of leftover scrubs
from the shopkeepers,
    the Bashiga house
    of Alhaji mai kudi
    the magnanimous eating mat
    of Alhaji Garba.
    The fura da nono
    Stand of Hajjia Binta
Like the constant
northern star
they never disappear
out of circulation
they are everywhere
what they search for is nowhere
but plenteous somewhere

like a measuring spectacle
they display their depravity

squalor and human decadence
In the open field
of a malevolent society
their eyes illuminate out
the depths of their crude
negligence and abandon

which ought to melt
even the hearts of granite
our affluence, their conflict
our food, their hunger
our happiness, their sadness
our drink, their thirst
our healthy, their ill
our peace, their pieces
our bliss, their blaze.

Their trauma ought to
pierce deep and cut
the esteem and dignity
of modest beings.

But are they shadows?
Shadows have no
residence
shadows flow and float
on space unfeeling.

They are not shadows
they are beautiful beings
born into unsensitive clan heads
who cannot see beyond
their eccentricity
a mundane clique
lording over a mundane society
whose sacrificial lamb
is the
Almajiri boy.

(September 1997)

"And in their wealth the beggers and needy have a right"– *Quran 51:19*

LORDS OF THE MANOR

He treks barefooted
on the scorching sand
criss crossing
the crest and trough
of his endangered space
in search of
crumbs on dumps.

His face
a mass of budding flies
caressing him passionately
their buzz music
to his sleepless ears
his body a host
to parasitic insects
which hug him passionately
himself a parasitic species
with licence to parasite on parasitables
under mai Abinci's bench
inside the market maze

he sleeps but rest awake
fighting off his adversaries
    hunger
    and
    flies
    his whole life a celebration of deprivation.

(September 1997)

"Like a visioner I knew that the almajiri system in the north is a time bomb waiting to explode. In my opinion the majority of youths and adults that found themselves in the Boko Haram of today are rebels of the system" – Kenn Amaechi Jnr.

Kenn Amaechi Jnr.

BORN TROWEY

My soulmates
I trowey salute
How una dey?

good luck and
long struggle
to you all
More grease to your elbow
less strain to your stress
may your pocket
be refilled with crumbs
may you all find
Naira and kobo
After errand or
a little queerness
with the Alhaji or madam
may your loot increase
After vandalisation in Ajegunle
                            Idumota
                            Sabongari
                            Upper Iweka

May the Police go blind
while you pick the
mallams large pocket
may you never be
kangarooed to death
by the irate mob
in the market who
does not know
that you bore a curse
from the womb.
And may you find
a shackle shelter
under the mainland bridge
if the ministry throws you out
may you be quartered
    covered

Orange Taste

under the blanket of night.

I
have come to join you
my mouth is dry
my stomach has shrunk
my buttocks are skeletal
I am a mini kwashiorkor
I walk but as a shadow
Among images.

My master Chief Ezego
threw me into a cell
for one kobo deficit on sales
The Police massacred me
with koboko and hunger
when I got drained
they threw me away
to the street
which I now
hug passionately.

Last night
I dreamt, I dreamt
a ghost dream
I saw my great grand papa
I saw my papa too
But I have never
Set my big eyes on
I saw them

    Along a narrow street
    where only a pin
    can pass up yonder
    descending and ascending
    they said to me
    go back, back to earth
    your time is not
    yet come.

Kenn Amaechi Jnr.

Here
I am before you
I come to be
troubadour I transverse
to seek your
blood union
to seek your
baptism of fire
so that I too can partake
of the spoil
    feed me
    fire me
    ignite me
then mould me
like an Iron
and let me
loose
    loose
like a cannon
into the cocoon
of a dirty
unfeeling society.

(January 1998)

"He that is good is free, though he is a slave; He that is evil is a slave though he be as king" – *Saint Augustine of Hippo*

Orange Taste

HUNGER, PAINS AND MISERY

I have seen and felt
misery, pain and hunger
I have been afflicted
With the triple horned evil
Once, twice and often
But I have seen and lived
in happiness and comfort
once, twice and often
and learnt excruciatingly
misery, pain and hunger
ain't the best of companions
but to the destitutes
they are the bride
that diffuse divorce.

     If
you have walked
barefooted in the Maiduguri
and Sokoto desert sun
    if
you have ever stayed unclothed
in the scotching harmattan of Yola
    if
you have been on your toes
running helter-skelter for shelter
while the heavens
pours their sentinels
in Kano and Potiskum plains
    if
you have ever roamed the streets
hungry, barefooted and ragged
    if
you have ever stayed
hungry, hopeless and despondent
    if
you have ever been
angry, sad and frustrated

Kenn Amaechi Jnr.

you will scream
the same song
I am croaking here
You will wail and cry
Out for God's mercy
for those human spectacles
I too have lived to be detached
I had cordoned off
flow of morbid emotions
that overwhelms me
at the sight of the
weeping child of misery
I had built a wall of separation
Between me and them
But the luster
Of humanness betrayed
My cosmetic demeanor
Like myself
I believe they are also humans
with rights, privileges and dignity
as the sacred law enshrines
and should be cared for
they should be let out of the streets
into natural sanctuaries
in homes and schools
within the embrace of
parental love, and friends
the plate-carrying heads
the tray-carrying heads the load carrying heads
the errand running foots
the human beasts of burden
should and must be
  regarded
  and restituted
  interregnum.
  (August 1997)

"The greatest good you can do for another is not just to share your riches but to reveal to him his own" – Benjamin Disraeli

Orange Taste

GIDAN VIDEO

In the town of Potiskum
the likes of gidan sani abound
where kindergarten children
and liberalised destitute
go to rest their wretched selves
with their eyes
magnetised to the
white man's box
in trance they watched
the show of life
opposite their life
they yelled and cheered
at the void in they soul.

Gidan video
is the training ground
for Universal Basic Education
for those kids and youths
they knowledge and civilisation
begins and ends
with the fantasies
from gidan video
talking pictures.

Gidan video
is the breeding ground
for communicable diseases,
breath and heat
flow unrestrained
though open roofed
the congestion
flame combustion.

Gidan video
is the love nest
that rears

Kenn Amaechi Jnr.

the incestuous courtship
of the juvenile and delinquent
into sad marriages
that hit the streets naked
on the eve of their
honey moon.

Gidan video
is a tempestous joy
out of a dark existence
in the dark alley
of ignorance
      and depravation.   (May 2002)

"It's only by avoiding the beginning of things that we can escape their ending" – *Unknown*

Orange Taste

THE INQUEST

A child seldom gives
What he never has
What he receives
He holds tights
One don't bequeath what he doesn't own
What you own you first appropriate
      Tell me
Does one export what he lacks?
      Or
Do one import what he has in abundance
It's only in darkness one search for light
An age long wisdom proclaims
Lanterns are not hidden under a basket.

I was told under my grandfather's feet
That a black goat
Is better searched in daytime
Because darkness is clothed
In a black skin.
Also where there is light
People find a path to follow
It is also said
That when the head of a fish is rotten
The body will be rotten too.
And when the eyes shed tears
The nostrils usually follow
But, I have head too
That fables, when repeated
Is accepted for the truth.

Tell me
Whether the parents malaise
Always affect the offspring's?

For I have seen
A son whose father is a sluggard
But the son valiant by choice

Kenn Amaechi Jnr.

I have seen too
A valiant tribe
Whose offspring are all cowards.

Is there a kingdom without king?
Is there a nation without leaders?
Is there a land without elders?
Even the ants have a king
        But
My people, our people
Have no king.
        no leaders
        no elders
Herein
Lives a tribe
Whose God is money
A people with so much knowledge
But a penny wise wisdom
A nation with so great a wealth
But lives in the wilderness
A state whose
Leaders have no followers
And followers leader-less.

Aro where are you?
Amadioha is this your wish?
Ikenga where is our ancestry?

A witch cry at night
Is a preamble to wailing
In the morning
And when a child cries
And point at a direction
The cause of his pain
 Is not far to fetch
Tell me now
Whether we were caused
To sow and never reap
And when we reap
We do so with tears…

Orange Taste

Tell me before I die
Why it never rain but pours
Why it never shines but dim
Why we live in strife
Why we toil in vain
Why our stars exeunt
Before they setting
      Tell me now
         Before I die
   Why the Igbos
     Wonders in wealth.

(2003)

Kenn Amaechi Jnr.

ACADEMIC RAZZMATAZZ

Look around
their bourgeois room
with a needle eye
you will see
they have all the antiquities
Arabian rugs
TV, video machines, CDs
And walled nude fixture
theirs is a cool
luxury dens
the symbol
of their superior
class in campus
a class of razzmatazzes

Yesterday
was a party spree
today
a rendezvous out campus
tomorrow
another jamboree
for hot jives and babes
to keep them in the move
they keep on cruising and craving
the aesthetic and temporary
they inspired cul-de-sac
till time fades.

But!
look around
search their I.Q.
a tabularasa of common sense
look at Dr? Kabir
MBBS? Final year
A graduate? Potentiate!
A scion of the emirate

Orange Taste

A future leader
a physician in the making
a doctor in the cracking
    watch and hear him
    He is empty of sense
    His voice is vacant
    of medical jargons and etiquette
    He is castrated
    of the medical organ
An infamy he shares
with Barri Obi?
Whose father
Is a business tycoon
An heir apparent to
the business empire
he knows not
of the Nigerian Legal System
fooling is freedom
in his wisdom
he reads law for fancy .
    Also Eng. Wale?
Engineer? B.Sc potentia?
his father
And honourable of the Senate.
Wale is a negation of
anything engineering science.
For them

    the ivory tower
    is a playground
    for the cocoanut head products
    of the breeds of our
    wasted generations
    who now sit in leadership
    of their wasted nation
    our conquered
apathetic fatherland.

    How be it

Kenn Amaechi Jnr.

Our future
their future alone
by waylaying
and intimidating
they break in steeply
into their father's
infamous shoes
to complete the rape
and rodent massacre
of the mother-land.

As for us
who eat voraciously
volumes of antiquated
waste materials
and sleep awake
with encyclopedias.
We that paint
our future
with holistic researches
we have dug out
answers to questions

fand in vacuous vacancies
our Guardian to punch
out our disparagement.

Those
That fortune smiled upon
from the crooked tables
of the lands overlords
join the coat and tie
wearing spectacles
on footwears in the streets
of Lagos, Kaduna and Port Harcourt
those that attract
the other face of fortune
end up
with hired cabs
rom the ground.

Orange Taste

Our flesh has
Stuck to our bones
to catch up with
lectures in
chilly harmattan halls
'smoking Garri'
with boiled beans
has become our
cherished delicacy
    oblivious
we move gaudily
with thoughts fixed
on wind fortunatus.
Our future
awaits us in the street

Molue and barbing salons
or go back
to the university
apprenticeship
of chief hope
carpentry workshop
for M.Sc.

(June 1999)

"The only truth that our leaders comprehend is the truth of the graveyard, If not they need not be told that Nigerian universities deserves a surgical operation" – Kenn Amaechi Jnr.

Kenn Amaechi Jnr.

BROKEN

Day after day
Night after night
Open eyed, we dream
Of the ivory tower.

The tower of knowledge
The tower of power
The tower of affluence
The tower of excellence

In reverence and thirst
We suspended sleep and sought perfection
In volume after volume of books
We browsed like termites
In haste to the tower.

Alas!
Academic prowess was usurped
For money prowess and mediocrities
Entrance becomes a vain dream
Except for the money bags.

Inside the tower
Hide and seek game take stead
Skirts and trousers flirt together
Cult and corruption courts
To give life to the yet stillborn degrees.
Outside the tower
Incompetency is unmasked
Mediocrity is unleashed
Dangerous literate parades
Confusion set in
And the tower, like the Babel
crashes from its roots.
Broken.

(February 1997)

Orange Taste

BAKASSI

    A relic
    of ancient memories
    is it?
        Yes but no.

    A remnant
    of refugee camp
    is it?
        Yes but no.

    The field of conflict?
    is it?
        Yes but no.
    Its a dim interstice
    amongst stars
    naked to desert scorching
    under the tower of shelter.

    A tragedy among glories
    A wretched wreck
    In the vast
    ocean of excellence.

    Our own bakassi
    an incandescent rows of faces
    the panoply of brilliant
    and intelligent dreamers
    creating careers
    from the hall of hopelessness

    Our own Bakassi
    A nauseating slum
    for nauseating adventure
    in quest for knowledge
    click clack of spoons
    shaff shaff of books

studies and cookery engaged
to give taste to tastelessness.

Our own bakassi
flowered with cul de sac
and fanned by mosquito wings
immune to the sweetness
of its bite.
the choking
of human waste and gutters

aroma of our breath
We sleep, but rest awake
dreaming thoughts
of an academic pandemonium.

(February 1997)
**Bakassi is the name for the slum-like, makeshift accommodation hall in the University of Maiduguri. It was originally a common room before it was converted to accommodation rooms because of lack of sleeping space for students.

Orange Taste

ECHOES OF CONSCIENCE

    At times and seasons
    In the hours and days
    When all senses became senile
    When men
        Angels and
        Deities
    In collaborative acquiescence
    Slaughtered reason
        Justice
        Equity
    At the alter of hedonistic
        Greed
        avarice
        and
        self ego
    Conscientious men of noble vision
    Has risen
    And stood in obeisance to truth
    Their voices has echoed
        reverberating
        breaking
    all the boundaries and barriers
    against the liberty of humanity
    and today as in the past
        present
        future
    mankind lives in reverence
        to the
        echoes of conscience

(May 2003)

For Martin Luther King and Nelson Mandela

Kenn Amaechi Jnr.

OGBANJE

Ogbanje

        Infant terrible
        Adult terror
        Tell me
        Who seared you
        Who mothered you
        Who sent you
        Tell me!

        You died long ago
        Decrees crucified you
        Abatcha buried you
        But here you come again
Ogbanje

        Tell me
        Who conceived you
        Asisi's loin is impotent
        His hot rod cooled down
        After a dozen of salary increment

        Tell me
        Who seared you
        Was it Fash?
        Who never got his share

        Tell me
        Ogbanje.
        Fash"s black dry dingy dick
        Seared you
        His insatiate thirst
        Gave you birth
        Now
        Tell me
        What do you want?
        To waste my generation more
        To throw mud and bricks

Orange Taste

On our thorn infested journey
To degree
Tell me
What do you seek
Fash don't love you
His desire is to wet his manhood
Give you birth to terror
And let you cry out malnutrition
While you weep
Fash romances federa
Takes home 20%
And dump you
To the undertakers
Fash and his ilk's
Like the famous osho baba
Are adolescent pimps.

Ogbanje
Go home to mother earth
She loves you dearly
Your memory will remain
Evergreen in our lives
We will honour you
With a statute of terror
At the gates of
Universities of Nigeria
An epitaph

Ogbanje strikes

R.I.P.
NANS

(April 2001)

"Most of the ASUU strikes were meant for personal aggrandizements, not for students' benefit or universities' growth. I experienced it all and this is my yestimony" – Kenn Amaechi Jnr.

NGIGE

The gods are fools
In the ways of men
If they are not
Man is but
 A dice in the palm
Of the gods.

From the foul
Of midnight's
Perfect contrivance
Comes the breath
Of the spirit

    Ngige
The spirit moves
In the consciousness
Of the people
Agrimesome memory
Of our leproit
Political culture.

    Ngige
The spirit moves
Unmasking
The nakedness
Of our leaders.

    Ngige
The spirit moves
In it's trails

The caricature
Of democracy

    Ngige
The spirit moves
Clothed

Orange Taste

In the rags

Of infamy.

Ngige
The spirit moves
A statute of greed
The spirit moves
A consuming storm.
The evil child
Of the merchants
Of voodo
      Now
A prince of the gods
To exorcise the consciousness
Of the people
And lay bear
The might of the mirror

Ngige
Whom the gods
Have called
A spirit of change
To clease the land
Of the shakle of greed
Ngige
Welcome home:

"When God will give an exceptionally Bright crown to a soul, he first of all impacts an exceptionally Heavy cross" – Anonymous

**Written on the 17th of July 2005, after a Supreme Court verdict restored the Anambra State Governorship mantle to Governor Chris Ngige.

Kenn Amaechi Jnr.

LONG LIVE THE KING

Our leaders
Have gone mad again!
No!
It is my pen that is mad.
It writes things, I don't understand
Can't you see?
The commander in chief
And the chorus men
Glowing in flamboyant agbada!

     Yes
they are not naked!
     Ah!
You can't fathom
My pen's confusion,

"I have got no soothsayer
I am natural
My ink writes clearly
And the message
Is of madmen, dancing in the square.

Have you not heard!
The drumming and dancing
Of the committee in lunacy.?

Have you not heard?
The songs of the
Chief guardian of the madmen?
Cant you hear the chorus?

Ijoya
Long life the king
Ijoya
Continual infinitum
Ijoya

Orange Taste

Till the kingdom come
Ijoya
And the land is quaked
Ijoya.

Our leaders have
Gone mad again…
Their sickness is contagious
The land await another
Healings
Of blood and bones
And the earth
Yielding its depths
In reception
Of our leaders
Who go on?
Contracting
Madcow disease"

"The windmills of the Gods
Grinds slowly, but it grinds
Exceedingly fine.
And he that the gods wants to kill they first make mad"
  – Yoruba adage

***Written on the 17th of July 2005 during the conflict between Olusegun Obasanjo and Atiku Abubakar towards the end of their presidency with each accusing the other of corruption and dishonesty and thereby causing heated political debates in Nigeria.*

Kenn Amaechi Jnr.

THE VERDICT

There was no drumbeat
Nor dancers of fortune
Neither trumpets of fortitude
At the echoes of justice
From Uwais' temple
Like the stolen mandate
So also the the verdict
delivered before sunrise
When all motive for mischief
Is charmed and cheifed,
The people were not surprised
They were amazed, but not fazed
For the comet- cometh
Before the raining storm.

We have seen before now
The eyes and trail of the godfathers
And the ambush of the gods
The falcon, is now the falconer
And midnight vow for avarice
Become the talk show of sunrise
And a soap opera at sunset
Fate and chance made love at dawn
And the people found their voice
In the spirit of a man
Voice populi, voice dei
No judgement by the junks can void it.

"When bad men combine, the goods must associate, else they fall, one after the other an unpiled sacrifice in a contemptible struggle."
     –   *Edmand Burke*

**Written on the 22nd of July *after a Supreme Court verdict restored the Anambra State Governorship mantle to Governor Chris Ngige*

Orange Taste

ASO ROCKS IS FALLING

Aso rock is cracking
The foundation is breaking
The roof is leaking
The walls are falling
the debris is splintering
The bond of the Niger.

Aso rock is cracking
The lord and his lordess
"Have murdered sleep"
They read the bible
And recite the Qur:an
All nigh till day break
So that, they reign
shall not end.

Aso rock is cracking
The foundation is falling
The land is rumbling
Because the emperor is rambling
That the khalifa is a rebel
He does not suck his breast
And message his back.
Aso rock is cracking
The roof is leaking
The beautiful marble
Is now poto –potoish
The smooth flowered road to 2007
Is overrun by potholes
And littered with thorns
The anointed, has disappointed.
Aso rock is cracking
The walls are falling
The lords of the manor
Are testing their manhood
in the puplic places

Kenn Amaechi Jnr.

They masturbate inside
The talking box
Yet they are insatiate.

Aso rock is cracking
The house is falling apart
The debris is splintering
The bond of the Niger

    But
The crack will not sink the people
It's our comic relief
To a dry fairly tale,
It is the day of the masses
To laugh and jeer
Till curtain fall
On the grand gladiators

(September 16, 2005)

Things have fallen apart
The center can no longer hold, the falcon has become the falconer
as mere anarchy, is upon the face of the
Earth.
    –   *Chinua Achebe (Things Fall Apart.)*

Written on the 17th of July 2005 during the conflict between Olusegun Obasanjo and Atiku Abubakar towards the end of their presidency with each accusing the other of corruption and dishonesty and thereby causing heated political debates in Nigeria.

Orange Taste

TO YOU

To you whose voice is still
When our people cry
To you whose face is unseen
In the mirror of our struggle
To you who has not lent a hands
To pull down the forces of oppression against our nation

To you who have not taken a step
To walk against injustice
To you who *siddon look* and hibernate
When action beckon against tyranny

To you who acquiesces to dine with falsehood
While truth is starved to extinction
To you whose politics and leadership
Is the gain and greed of your avarice
To you who answered *the-come-and-chop* diner with traitors
And sacrificed your dignity like Esau at our tormentors table

To you that failed to stand up for truth, justice and equity
And doeth nothing while the merchants of oppression, tyranny
And capitalist hawks maimed our people
And plundered our fatherland

Know you that pestilence has no favorite
And the wrath of our Gods
Shall be roughed on you
till your memory fade eternally.

History will have to record that the greatest tragedy of this period of social transition was not the strident clamor of the bad people, but the appalling silence of the good people
– Martin Luther King Jnr.

Kenn Amaechi Jnr.

MY COUNTRY FINE

My country fine well well
Everywhere na so so oil
Inside the ground and on the trees
But our people can not
Pay for the price of oil

My country fine well well
Plenty plenty things e dey
Cocoa, gypsum, and silver e dey
But my people eyes kolo
Na only white men dey see
And take the plenty better things
Wey dey for my country

My country fine well well
All my people will go to heaven
To meet God their father
Whom dem like well well
My country men
Have many churches and mosque
But in my country, our people
Eat their neighbor's wife
For nocturnal dinners
Steal their neighbor's goat
At the wink of dawn
And rich man's thirst na only poor man water dey quench am
The law in my country
Catches only the poor man

My country fine well well
Our leaders' deys lead us well well
From the top of the rock
All our resources go up to the rock
E no dey come back
Dey rock dey solid well well

Orange Taste

My country fine well well
Everything e dey
Petrol e dey , food e dey, money e dey
Everything boku for nija
But our people waka naked
Dem stomach sing songs at night
And dem like to pick and chop
Bad bad yamma yamma food from dust bin
Say food na food as them no wan fight government
For dem own right to good life because
Dem own time go kom for them to steal too

Dem dream to live long
But dem act to die quick
Because dem carry hope
Put inside body
Say dem go go to
Heaven with their white garment sins.
(August 2007)

"Nigerians are rated the most religious nation in the world, yet the most morally corrupt in their socio economic dealings – Kenn Amaechi Jr.

LOOT AND GO

Once upon a time
In the seasons of sleaze
On the hillside and plains
Of my fatherland
Reigneth
Baba Segun
And the 36 thieves
In the corridors of corruption
Looting and lusting
On our heritages
They ravaged our patrimony
Amongst their common fiends
And mortgaged our life assurance
To their loin pleasure
They fouled the air we breathe
And imprisoned our land
With their unconscient lust
Of the of the flesh and its vanities
Today
At the gate of judgment
Our only arch angel
Mallam Riba-bad
The mallam of prudence
And their lordships
Have become Father Christmas
With our prized xmas hampers
Dashing them a taste of the jail house
And a plea
For their bargain
They said
Its loot and goo

*Written after the harvest of corruption cases against the governors of the Third Republic. Most of the cases ended in plea bargains, whereby the governors declares a fraction of their loots and the courts set them free

MY MISSING MUSE

My muse has missed
My ink has ceased to flow
My line is blank
My mind too has gone bland
My thoughts are touchy
As I think of a line and a song
        Fit
For the great arraignment
My muse, has missed
The drops of turakis tears
The coldness of Dariyees skin
The dampness of Nyameees Agbada
The acrobats of Nnamanes heart beat
The delusion of Kaluus bragadoo
At the great arraignment
The irokos of graft whose states money
Became their patrimony
Perfidy and avarice
A celebration of eccentric passions
Have come to the temple of retribution
To offer testimonials of their common crimes

My muse have missed
My ink seized to flow
My thoughts searches for a song
To express the awesome fall
Of yesterdays men of unbridled power
From the heights of vanities
In the great arraignment.

**Written in 2007 after hand over of government by ex-Governors of the Third Republic and their various arraignment on corruption charges.

Kenn Amaechi Jnr.

TURAKI WEPT

Turaki wept
Not because
Of his impoverished talakawas
That he sleazed
Their flesh and blood
And left them stricken
In malnutrition
In his eight years
Of mis adventure
Turaki wept
Not because his conscience called
At the hour of retribution
To exorcise him
Of the guilt of avarice

Turaki wept
Not because
Of the shame of infamy
That lifted the veil
Of his crude criminalities
Against the humanity
Of his people

Turaki wept
Not because
Of the wraths of the sharia
And the loss
Of AL-Jennah

Turaki wept
Because the key to sleaze
And the shade of corruption
Is seized from him.
(2007)

**Turaki is an ex-governor of one of the northern states. He ruled from 1999 to 2007.

Orange Taste

WE KNOW

      We know
    Who gave you birth
   You are the spawn
Of a leproutic political godfather
But
We know too that your bloodline
Is of a virtues genealogy
We know
You stink
We can feel the foul smell
Of your white garment agbada
We are choked by the odor
Emanating from your stolen crown
Gathering koro koro flies
On your fine egg head
The burden of
A stolen mandate

We too
We feel your pain
And we hurt with you
We know
Your spirits is weakened
But your manhood is strong
Though you hang a smile
We can see the smear
That is your honor
We are aggrieved
Not because of your tainted crown
We are aggrieved
Because our will have been amputated
Our pride and honour
Smitten
And we dare not cry out
Hence ehindero crush us like tomatoes

Kenn Amaechi Jnr.

In your pain we despair
In your grieve we groin
But our nation must be healed
So
Do the rituals
And calm the goddess of anger
Then
Take our hands
Make the sacrifice
And excoriate the land
Of all locust, vipers
And greedy cannibals
Masquerading as leaders
We love you
And our love will lead you
To the place of our heart
To do good to all our people
Uncle Umaru Musa Yar'adua.

**Written around 2p.m. on 29th may, 2007 after Umaru Musa Yar'adua's inauguration.*

Orange Taste

TAKE THE OATH

Take the oath
Don't die by the letters
But live the worlds
The constitution
Your sacred volition.
Proclaim the allegiance
The letters are words
The words truth
The truth
That holds the promise
Of a greater nation.
Open your heart
Listen to the anthem
And hearken to the sanctity of the pledge
The Siamese bond
Of a people bound
By a common destiny
Do make the speech
It is the tradition
But
Do not follow in the vain customs
Of our Herods past
Who betrayed our destinies
To the altar of vanities.
Open your heart
To the quest of the commoners
Lend your hands to the creation
Of a fresh nation
Listen to the voices of the people
Your people, our people
And do …
The will of GOD!
**Written on the 29th of May 2009 to Uncle Umaru Musa Yar'adua, after his Inauguration as President.

Kenn Amaechi Jnr.

LET'S MOVE FORWARD AGAIN

Let's move forward
Though the scars and brubt
Of an april fools day election
Remain ingrained in your memory
Like a sore in the scrotum

Let's move forward
Though our carriage
Carries a bad baggage
Proceeds of a day light robbery
Of the painful gains of our labor
For a government of the people
Lost to bandits of power

Let's move forward
Though the gatherings storms
Stills our hopes
And the hanging cloud
Calls our doubts
I see faith
in the eyes of the storm
In the clouds
I see the glamour
Of rainbow rising

Let's move forward
Though our steps are chameleonic
And our locomotion
The speed of a millipede
With courage
We will reach our destination

**Written in June 2007, a month after Yar'adua's swearing-in. There was mass riots and killings in the North, especially in Kano in protest of the election result.

Orange Taste

GLORY PLACE

Doom
Bomb
Blast
Bang
Freedom shall walk tall
Seamlessly in all season
In our land

Rain
Sun
Storm
Earthquake
Heaven quake
Liberty shall be the citadel
Of our people

Hunger
Hate
Strife
Pain
Peril
Commotions
Emotions
Siege
Sentiments
Justice shall be enthroned
On the earth like
Waters cover the seas
In our land

Transformation
Changes
Bokos
Harams
Chibok

Kenn Amaechi Jnr.

Girls
Troop
Threat
Terror
Tears
The truth crushed down to earth
Shall rise again
And reign in the deepest
Weakness and strength
Of Nigeria and Nigerians.

(January 2011)

"I'm an incurable optimist in the Nigerian project. I believe that, irrespective of our various legendary differences and intermittent emotional conflicts, Nigeria and Nigerians will always rise up to unite for the good of the Nation and for the unity of our country" – Kenn Amaechi Jr.

Orange Taste

I SEE HOPE

I see hope
I see hope
In the meek eyes
Of uncle Yar' adua
Not the ephemeral hope
I saw in the haughty and hollow years
Of Baba Segun and the 36 thieves

I see hope in the gentle but gallant
Steps of uncle yar, aduas
Redemptive mission
In this land of blind and lost vision

I see hope
Spread over our horizons
Like the stars of Abraham
Shinning down on the
Dry dreams of Nigerians
Decapitated fountain
Uncle Yar' adua
Is on the throne
Rulling with the rule of law.

**Written on the 1st Oct, 2007 after Yar'adua's swearing in. My hope in Yar'adua was later wrestled away by the force of death. May he rest in peace.

Kenn Amaechi Jnr.

I HAVE A DREAM

I have a dream
Like Joseph dreamt
And famished Israel
Found nourishment
In pharaohs store house
In the season of desolation

I have a dream
Like martin luther dreamt
And segregated America
Became intergrated
As the Caucasoid and negroid
Became one under God
And today we have
     OBAMA.

I have a dream
Like Awo, Zik, and Balewa dreamt
Of a great Nigeria
And built the foundation
Of a prosperous nation.

I have a dream
That the ashes
And the sparkle of the stars
Like the dawn of sunrise
Of our inglorious past shall manure the rebirth
Of a great nation
With an auction
To function
In fulfillment of our dreams
Of life more abundant

**Written after the dawn of Yar'adua's Presidency on the 10th of August 2007

Orange Taste

YOU LOST YOUR GROOVE

You lost your groove
When you let the maddening crowd
That hears only the songs of their poverty
From the beats of your enemies
Stampede you to throw away the nozzle against subsidy.

Night has dawned, morning is nigh
The philosophers and slave masters
That reigned you into submission
Are the choirmasters that sings
Another lewd song of subsidy
And the maddening crowd are dancing in limbo.

You lost your groove
When you cried like a sheep
That you are not a lion
And need not roar to soar
Your mind was lost to the allure of the commoners
   The charm of the roaring lion!
      The lion king of the jungle!
         Who cuddle her own with tenderness
           And bundle her preys to extinction
              To prove the steeliness of her Manhood.

You lost your groove uncle Jonathan
When you let the marauding BOKOS and their HARAMIST
Poke their filthy furious demented fingers
On our little effervescent angels
And ruptured their virgin innocence
With their savage uncircumcised M16 & sordid bombs
On the rusty desert of CHIBOK
They were carried in the dark like frost in the wind
Into SAMBISA foul forest
And their petals cruelly fractured
Their beauty burnt to ashes and their innocence defiled.

Kenn Amaechi Jnr.

Our girls are still in the wind
And what we can remember is your denial that they were never lost
You lost it with our girls in the terrorist den
As the cupid shouts on the streets ....
BRING BACK OUR GIRLS!!!

You lost your groove
When you fought petty on the street of public opinion
With your ex governors colleagues
You took a pyrrhic victory over a cap on a crownless head
And lost your universal fatherhood over the governors
 And because Amaechi Rotie has nothing to lose
He made your erections seems like a steam less wagon
And laid your potency castrate amidst your cheerleader's.

You lost your groove
When you told our many unlearned citizens
That "stealing is not corruption"
In their common sense, your wisdom was loose
For stealing to the common man is corruption
Your scientific annihilation of corruption is crack to them
Because their Pharaoh past
Whom they now fantasize was wise
To hang the chicken thief in the public place
And grant a bed rest to the scientific looters.

You lost your groove
Your charms lose its fragrance
And your aura went with the wind
Yesterday you were a bloom shining freshness of dew
Today a staleness that chocks
Even your passionate of lovers
Your spark and glow is like that of a fermented whore
Standing Alone
In the glitz of darkness......

Orange Taste

**Written in April 2015 after the incumbent president Goodluck Ebele Jonathan lost the 2015 presidential election to Gen. Muhammadu Buhari.

Kenn Amaechi Jnr.

THE QUIET TEMPEST

    Like a quiet tempest
    That stood still
    In the storm of a fairy whirlwind
    At the setting of the sun
    The people roused their anger against
    The odious baggage's of the umbrella party
    And with their thumps and in their rage
    threw away the umbrella cleavages
    Into the calm but roaring sea of ignominy
    Yet the tempest was quietened
    because the gods have pre ordained the day;
    The battle for change was won amidst the cloud
    That heralded a new dawn that calmed
    The ferocious whirlwind of change

(April 2015)

Written after the 2015 Election …

Orange Taste

CRY, BELOVED SENIOR SCIENCE POTISKUM YOBE STATE

At that assembly ground, I baked my wit with words
And sharpened my passion for grammar
Every Monday morning was a day to glow
And walk with adolescent swag that
Lift my feet high and makes my arms swing like the wing of a high flying eagle above the stars
And as I read out the news for the week, the silence and attention makes me immortal and god like
Amidst my adoring worshippers.

I was the assembly newscaster
Isa Abdullah was often the lead newscaster
We could have been amongst the death if today is 1995

At that assembly ground dreams were built and destiny casted
In omniscient hope by the iron hand of Mr. Gimba
And the steel intergrity of mallam Jalo.
We were boys taught to be men
Tongue, tribe and faith differed
But we were one big happy family
In pursuit of life most precious call
The quest for knowledge
We could have been amongst the death if today is 1995

We could have been amongst the death if today is 1995
By providence today is 2014, many years gone
Today,
The assembly ground stands but in desolation
The assembly ground stands in pain
The assembly ground stands in sorrow
The assembly ground stands in tears
The assembly ground stands in blood
The blood of the knowledge seeking hopeful young children
Defiled and desecrated by goats with auto instinctive capacity
To bomb and to kill the innocent and the vulnerable
These goats are called BOKO HARAM .

Kenn Amaechi Jnr.

May our God brings judgment against boko haramist and their sympathizers
May our God grants peace and aljanafirdausi to the faithful departed
May our God grant our leaders the strength to defeat Boko Haram

Rest in Peace brothers!
Cry beloved Senior Science Potiskum yobe state.

**Written after Boko Haram suicide bomb attacked my Alma Mater government Senior Science Secondary School Potiskum on the 9th of October, 2014.

Orange Taste

SACRIFICE

    Sacrifice Is self-denial for others good
    Sacrifice is not giving out of your abundance
    Sacrifice is sharing the little you have
    Sacrifice is not giving in order to receive back
    Sacrifice is letting go whole-heartedly with no string attached
    Sacrifice is not doing it because you know him
    Sacrifice is doing it to whoever that needs it
    Sacrifice is not acting at your own convenience
    Sacrifice is inconveniencing yourself for others sake
    Sacrifice is not pretentious or boastful
    Sacrifice is humble and eager to please
    Sacrifice is not blowing your trumpet loud
    Sacrifice is allowing others to appreciate your worth's
    Sacrifice is not emotional or sentimental
    Sacrifice is love let loose on humanity
    Sacrifice is not acting to please man
    Sacrifice is acting to please God.
                        (2003)

    To a heart full of grace
        to a mind very humane
          to a spirit that inspires
            to a hand that lends
              to a man whose call
                is sacrifice
                  to

Thomas AquinasNwanze

Kenn Amaechi Jnr.

IT SHALL PASS OVER: A Poem for PMB

It hurts to hit hard
At whom we love
We gloss over the pain we bear
And see it as a sacrifice
For the love we share

Even when our hope is despaired
And our expectation impaired
With a faint heart and humbled faith
We look up to the icon of our devotion
To redeem our volution
And change the dark cloud over our change.

We shall not wail with the wailing wailers
Because we Love you and believe
As the days of cluelessness passed away
So also these days of economic cruelties
Shall pass over!

**For President Mohammadu Buhari , May 2016

Orange Taste

"We hold these truth to be self evident that all men are created equal that they are endowed by their creator with certain inalienable rights, that amongst these right are life, liberty and the pursuits of happiness... even if expressed in verses of poetry" – **Thomas Jefferson**

www.ingramcontent.com/pod-product-compliance
Lightning Source LLC
Chambersburg PA
CBHW051346040426
42453CB00007B/437